ONCE

Books by Alice Walker

The Color Purple
Goodnight, Willie Lee, I'll See You in the Morning
*I Love Myself When I Am Laughing
A Zora Neale Hurston Reader (editor)*
In Love & Trouble
In Search of Our Mothers' Gardens
Langston Hughes, American Poet
Meridian
Once: Poems
Revolutionary Petunias and Other Poems
The Third Life of Grange Copeland
You Can't Keep a Good Woman Down

once

POEMS BY

ALICE WALKER

A Harvest/HBJ Book
Harcourt Brace Jovanovich, Publishers
San Diego   New York   London

Library of Congress Cataloging in Publication Data

Walker, Alice, date
Once.

(A Harvest book ; HB 337)
I.   Title.
PS3573.A42505   1976   811'.5'4   75-29307
ISBN 0-15-668745-3   *(Harvest/HBJ : pbk.)*

D   E   F   G   H   I   J

For Howard Zinn

Poverty was not a calamity for me. It was always balanced by the richness of light . . . circumstances helped me. To correct a natural indifference I was placed half-way between misery and the sun. Misery kept me from believing that all was well under the sun, and the sun taught me that history wasn't everything.

—Albert Camus, *De l'envers et l'endroit*

CONTENTS

ONCE

AFRICAN IMAGES

Glimpses from a Tiger's Back

i

Beads around
my neck
Mt. Kenya away
over pineappled hills
Kikuyuland.

ii

A book of poems
Mt. Kenya's
Bluish peaks
"Wangari!"*
My new name.

iii

A green copse
And hovering
Quivering
Near our bus
A shy gazelle.

** Kikuyu clan name indicating
honorary acceptance into the
Leopard clan.*

iv

morning mists
On the road
an Elephant
He knows
his rights.

v

A strange noise!
"Perhaps an elephant
is eating our roof"
In the morning
much blue.

vi

A tall warrior
and at his feet
only
Elephant bones.

vii

Elephant legs
In a store
To hold
Umbrellas.

viii

A young man
Puts a question
In his language
I invariably
End up
Married.

ix

The clear Nile
A fat crocodile
Scratches his belly
And yawns.

x

The rain forest
Red orchids—glorious!
And near one's eyes
The spinning cobra.

xi

A small boat
A placid lake
Suddenly at one's hand
Two ears—
Hippopotamus.

xii

An ocean of grass
A sea of sunshine
And near my hand
Water buffalo.

xiii

See! through the trees!
A leopard in
the branches—
No, only a giraffe
Munching his dinner.

xiv

Fast rapids
Far below
Begins
The lazy Nile.

xv

A silent lake
Bone strewn banks
Luminous
In the sun.

xvi

Uganda mountains
Black soil
White snow
And in the valley
Zebra.

xvii

African mornings
Are not for sleeping
In the early noon
The servant comes
To wake me.

xviii

Very American
I want to eat
The native food—
But a whole goat!

xix

Holding three fingers
The African child
Looked up at me
The sky was very
Blue.

xx

In the dance
I see a girl
Go limp
"It is a tactic"
I think.

xxi

"America!?"   "Yes."
"But you are like
my aunt's cousin
who married so-and-so."
"Yes, (I say), I know."

xxii

On my knees
The earringed lady
Thinks I'm praying
She drops her sisal
and runs.

xxiii

"You are a Negro?"
        "Yes"
"But that is a kind
of food—isn't it—
the white man used to

eat you???"
     "Well—"

xxiv

Unusual things amuse us
A little African girl
Sees my white friend
And runs
She thinks he wants her
For his dinner.

xxv

The fresh corpse
Of a white rhinoceros
His horn gone
Some Indian woman
Will be approached
Tonight.

xxvi

The man in the
Scarlet shirt
Wanted to talk
but had no words—
I had words
but no Scarlet
Shirt.

xxvii

floating shakily down the
nile
on my rented raft
I try to be a native
queen
a prudent giraffe
on the bank
turns up
      his nose.

xxviii

We eat Metoke*
with three fingers—
other things
get two fingers
and one of those
a thumb.

xxix

That you loved me
I felt sure
Twice you asked
me gently
if I liked the
strange

* *A food staple of the Buganda*
in Uganda, made from plantains.

gray
stew.

xxx

Pinching both my legs
the old man kneels
before me on the
ground
his head white
Ah! Africa's mountain
peaks
Snow to grace
eternal spring!

xxxi

To build a hut
One needs mud
and sisal
And friendly
Neighbors.

xxxii

Where the glacier was
A lake
Where the lake is
Sunshine
And redheaded
Marabou storks.

xxxiii

On a grumpy day
An African child
Chants "good morning"
—I have never seen
Such bright sun!

xxxiv

The Nairobi streets
At midnight
Deserted
The hot dog man
Folds up his cart.

xxxv

In Nairobi
I pestered an
Indian boy to
Sell me a
Hat
For five shillings—
How bright
His eyes were!

xxxvi

In a kunzu
Long and white

Stands my African
Dad
The sound of drums
Fills
The air!

xxxvii

On my brother's motorcycle
The Indian mosques
And shops fade behind us
My hair takes flight
He laughs
He has not seen such hair
Before.

xxxviii

An African girl
Gives me a pineapple
Her country's national
Flower
How proudly she
Blinks the eye
Put out
By a sharp pineapple
Frond.
I wonder if I should
Kneel
At her bare little
Feet?

xxxix

At first night
I sat alone
& watched the
        sun set
behind
    the
aberdares
    During
     the day
         my legs
and the sun
    belonged
        to
     the village
         children.

xl

Under the moon
luminous
huts. . . .
Brown breasts stuck
out to taunt
the sullen wind.

xli

A crumbling
hut . . .

in the third
room
a red chenille
bedspread
(by Cannon)
a cracked
jar
of violet
    lilies
      (by?)

xlii

The native women
thought me
strange
until they
saw me follow you
to your hut.

xliii

In Kampala
the young king
goes often
to Church
the young girls here
are
So pious.

xliv

Settled behind
tall banana trees
the little hut
is overcovered by
their leaves
patiently it waits
for autumn
which never comes. . . .

xlv

in my journal
I thought I could
capture
everything. . . .
Listen!
the soft wings of cranes
sifting the salt sea
air.

LOVE

i

A dark stranger
My heart searches
Him out
"Papa!"

ii

An old man in white
Calls me "mama"
It does not take much
To know
He wants me for
His wife—
He has no teeth
But is kind.

iii

The American from
Minnesota
Speaks Harvardly
of Revolution—
Men of the Mau Mau
Smile
Their fists holding
Bits of
Kenya earth.

iv

A tall Ethiopian
Grins at me
The grass burns
My bare feet.

v

Drums outside
My window
Morning whirls
In
I have danced all
Night.

vi

The bearded Briton
Wears a shirt of
Kenya flags
I am at home
He says.

vii

Down the hill
A grove of trees
And on this spot
The magic tree.

viii

The Kenya air!
Miles of hills
Mountains
And holding both
My hands
A Mau Mau leader.

ix

And in the hut
The only picture—
Of Jesus

x

Explain to the
Women
In the village
That you are
Twenty
And belong—
To no one.

KARAMOJANS

i

A tall man
Without clothes
Beautiful
Like a statue
Up close
His eyes
Are running
Sores.

ii

The Noble Savage
Erect
No shoes on his
feet
His pierced ears
Infected.

iii

"Quite incredible—
your hair-do is
most divine——
Held together
With *cow* dung?
You mean——?!

The lady stares
At her fingers.

iv

A proper English meal
Near the mountains
"More tea, please"
Down the street
A man walks
Quite completely
Nude.

v

Bare breasts loose
In the sun
The skin cracked
The nipples covered
With flies
But she is an old
Woman
What?—twenty?

vi

A Catholic church
The chaste cross
Stark
Against the purple sky.

We surprise a
couple there alone
In prayer?

vii

There is no need for
Sadness
After the dying boy
There is the living girl
Who throws you a
kiss.

viii

How bright the little
girl's
Eyes were!
a first sign of
Glaucoma.

ix

The Karamojans
Never civilized
A proud people
I think there
Are
A hundred left.

ONCE

i

Green lawn
a picket fence
flowers—
My friend smiles
she had heard
that Southern
jails
were drab.

Looking up I see
a strong arm
raised
the Law
Someone in America
is being
protected
             (from me.)

In the morning
there was
a man in grey
but the sky
was blue.

ii

"Look at that
nigger with those
white folks!"
　　My dark
Arrogant friend
turns calmly, curiously
helpfully,
　　　"Where?" he
　　　　asks.

It was the fifth
arrest
In as many
　　days
How glad I am
that I can
look
surprised
　　　　still.

iii

Running down
Atlanta
　　　streets
With my sign
I see heads
　　　turn
Eyes

       goggle
"a nice girl
    like her!"

A Negro cook
assures
        her mistress—

But I had seen
the fingers
near her eyes
    wet with
        tears.

iv

One day in
Georgia
Working around
the Negro section
My friend got a
letter
in
the mail
—the letter
said
        "I hope you're
having a good
time
fucking all
        the niggers."

"Sweet," I winced.
          "Who
               wrote it?"

"mother."
          she
               said.

That day she sat
          a long time
a little black girl
in pigtails
on her lap

Her eyes were very
Quiet.

She used to tell the big colored ladies
her light eyes just
the same
"I am alone
my mother died."
Though no other
letter
came.

v

It is true—
I've always loved

the daring
           ones
Like the black young
man
Who tried
to crash
All barriers
at once,
      wanted to
swim
At a white
beach (in Alabama)
Nude.

vi

Peter always
thought
the only
way to
"enlighten"
southern towns
was to
introduce
      himself
to
the county
sheriff
      first thing.

Another thing
Peter wanted—
was to be
cremated
　　but we
couldn't
　　find him
when he needed it.

But he was just a yid
　　seventeen.

　　vii
　　I
never liked
white folks
　　really
　　it
happened quite
　　suddenly
　　one
　　day
A pair of
　　amber
　　eyes
　　I
　　think
　　he
　　had.

viii

I *don't* think
  integration
    entered
      into it
        officer

You see
  there was
    this little
      Negro
       girl
Standing here
  alone
  and her
    mother
      went into
  that store
    there

then—
  there came by
this little boy
  here
without his
  mother
& eating
  an
ice cream cone
—see there it is—
  strawberry

Anyhow

      and the little
        girl was
        hungry
        and
        stronger
        than
        the little
        boy—

Who is too
   fat
  really,

      anyway.

ix

Someone said
     to
        me
that
    if
      the South
rises
    again
it will do so
   "from
the grave."

Someone
        else
                said
if the South
   rises
        again
he would
        "step on
            it."

Dick Gregory
   said that
      if the
         South
            rises
         again
      there is
         a
      secret
      plan.

But I say—
   if the
            South
rises
      again
It will not
   do
      so
in my presence.

x

"but I don'
really
        give a fuck
Who
   my daughter
     marries—"
the lady
was
adorable—
it was in a
tavern
i remember
her daughter
sat there
beside her
tugging
at
her arm
sixteen—
very shy
            and
very pim
            pled.

xi

then there
was
the charming
        half-wit

who told
the judge
re: indecent exposure
"but when I
step out
   of the
   tub
I look
   Good—
just because
my skin
is black
don't mean
it ain't
pretty
            you old bastard!)
what will we
finally do
with
prejudice

some people like
to take a walk
after a bath.

xii

"look, honey
said
the
blond

amply
boobed
babe
in the
green
  g
string

"i like you
sure
i ain't
prejudiced

but the
lord didn't
give me
legs
like
these
because
he
wanted
to see'm
dangling
from a
poplar!"

"But they're so
    much
        prettier
            than mine.

Would you really mind?"
he asked
wanting her to dance.

xiii

I remember
seeing
a little girl,
dreaming—perhaps,
  hit by
    a
van truck

"That nigger was
in the way!" the
man
    said
     to
understanding cops.

      But was she?
     She was
       just eight
        her mother
        said
     and little
         for
       her age.

xiv

then there was
the
picture of
the
bleak-eyed
little black
girl
waving the
american
flag
holding it
gingerly
with
the very
tips
of her
fingers.

CHIC FREEDOM'S

REFLECTION

(for Marilyn Pryce)

One day
Marilyn marched
beside me (demon-
stration)
and we ended up
at county farm
no phone
no bail
something about
"traffic vio-
lation"
which irrelevance
Marilyn dismissed
with a shrug
    She
had just got
    back
from
    Paris France
       In
    the
    Alabama
      hell
    she

smell-
ed
so
wonderful
like spring
& love
&
freedom

She
wore a
SNCC pin
right between
her breasts
near her
heart
& with a chic
(on "jail?")
accent
& nod of
condescent
to frumpy
work-house
hags
powdered her nose
tip-
toe
in a badge.

SOUTH:

THE NAME OF HOME

i

all that night
I prayed for eyes to see again
whose last sight
had been
a broken bottle
held negligently
in a racist
fist
God give us trees to plant
and hands and eyes to
love them.

ii

When I am here again
the years of ease between
fall away
The smell of one
magnolia
sends my heart running
through the swamps.

iii

the earth is red
here—
the trees bent, weeping
what secrets will not
the ravished land
reveal
of its abuse?

iv

an old mistress
of my mother's
gives me
bloomers for christmas
ten sizes
too big
her intentions are
good my father
says
but typical—
neither the color
she knows
nor the
    number.

HYMN

I well remember
A time when
"Amazing Grace" was
All the rage
In the South.
'Happy' black mothers arguing
Agreement with
Illiterate sweating preachers
Hemming and hawing blessedness
Meekness
Inheritance of earth, e.g.,
Mississippi cotton fields?

And in the North
Roy Hamilton singing
"What is America to me?"
Such a good question
From a nice slum
In North Philly.

My God! the songs and
The people and the lives
Started here—
Weaned on 'happy' tears
Black fingers clutching black teats
On black Baptist benches—
Some mother's troubles that everybody's
Seen
And nobody wants to see.

I can remember the rocking of
The church
And embarrassment
At my mother's shouts
Like it was all—'her happiness'—
Going to kill her.
My father's snores
Punctuating eulogies
His loud singing
Into fluffy grey caskets
A sleepy tear
In his eye.

Amazing Grace
How sweet the sound
That saved a wretch
Like me
I once was lost
But now I'm found
Was blind
But now
I see.

Mahalia Jackson, Clara Ward, Fats Waller,
Ray Charles,
Sitting here embarrassed with me
Watching the birth
Hearing the cries
Bearing witness
To the child,
Music.

THE DEMOCRATIC ORDER:

SUCH THINGS IN TWENTY YEARS

I UNDERSTOOD

My father
(back blistered)
beat me
because I
could not
stop crying.
He'd had
enough 'fuss'
he said
for one damn
voting day.

THEY WHO FEEL DEATH

(for martyrs)

They who feel death close as a breath
Speak loudly in unlighted rooms
Lounge upright in articulate gesture
Before the herd of jealous Gods

Fate finds them receiving
At home.

Grim the warrior forest who present
Casual silence with casual battle cries
Or stand unflinchingly lodged

In common sand
Crucified.

ON BEING ASKED TO LEAVE

A PLACE OF HONOR FOR ONE

OF COMFORT; PREFERABLY

IN THE NORTHERN

SUBURBS

*(for those who work and stay in the
ragged Mississippis of the world)*

In this place of helmets and tar
the anxious burblings of recreants
buzz over us
we bent laughing to oars of gold

We regard them as Antigone her living kin

Fat chested pigeons
resplendent of prodigious riches
reaped in body weight
taking bewildered pecks
at eagles
as though *muck*
were God.

THE ENEMY

in gray, scarred Leningrad
a tiny fist unsnapped to show
crumpled heads
of pink and yellow flowers
snatched hurriedly on the go
in the cold spring shower—

consent or not
countries choose
cold or hot
win or lose
to speak of wars
yellow and red
but there is much
let it be said
for children.

COMPULSORY

CHAPEL

i

A quiet afternoon
the speaker
dull
the New Testament
washed out
Through the window
a lonely
       blue-jay
makes noisy song.

ii

The speaker crashes
on
through his speech
All eyes are
upon him
Over his left
ear
the thick hair
is beginning
to slip.

iii

I would not mind
    if I were

                a sinner,

but as it is
—let me assure you—
I sleep alone.

TO THE MAN

IN THE YELLOW TERRY

Dawn came at six today
Held back by hope
A lost cause—
Melted like snow
In the middle of
The day.

The sun shines clear fire
The earth once more
Like it was—
Old promises
Rise up
(Our honored
        Ghosts)
And the lonely truths
Of love
Pledged.

Here we lie
You and I—
Your mind, unaccountable,
My mind simply
Stopped—
Like a clock struck
By the treachery
Of time.

The sky blue, empty,
Unfathomable—
As I am.
Look at it brighten
And fill and
Astonish
With each movement
Of your
Eyes.

The wren who does not
Sing
I take my simple
Flight
Silent, unmetaphoric
Dressed in brown
I say
Good-bye.

Will you think it funny
Later on
To find you had
Almost
Given shelter
To a
Thief?

THE KISS

i was kissed once
by a beautiful man
all blond and
           czech
riding through bratislava
on a motor bike
screeching "don't yew let me fall off heah naow!"

the funny part was
he spoke english
and setting me gallantly
on my feet
kissed me for
not anyhow *looking*
like aunt jemima.

WHAT OVID

TAUGHT ME

What does it matter? you ask
  If protocol
        falls
    After artichokes
      and steak,
        Vivaldi
          and
        No
        Wine

For God's sake
Let's not be traditional!

        But I,
      Unused bed
        All tousled
    Sing nursery rhymes
        Chant
          Strange
            Chants

    Count stray insects
    On the ceiling
          and
      Wonder—

Why don't you shut up and
                    get in?

MORNINGS / *of an impossible love*

On the morning you woke beside me—already thinking of going away—the sun did not fill my window as it does most mornings. Instead there was cloud and threat of snow. How I wish it could always be this way—that on mornings he cannot come himself, the sun might send me you.

Watching you frown at your face in the mirror this
morning I almost thought you disapproved of the little
dark shadow standing behind you its arms around your
waist. . . .

Two mornings ago you left my little house. Only two steps from my fingers & you were gone, swallowed down swiftly by my spiral stairs. . . .

Why do you wish to give me over to someone else? "Such and such young man you're sure to like" you say "for he is a fine, cheerful fellow, very sensitive" and one thing and another. Sometimes it is as if you'd never listened to my heartbeat, never heard my breathing in your ear, never seen my eyes when you say such things. . . .

This is what you told me once. Must I believe you? "We are really Easterners, you and I. The rising of the Sun brings with it our whole Philosophy."

SO WE'VE COME

AT LAST

TO FREUD

Do not hold my few years
                    against me
In my life, childhood
                    was a myth
So long ago it seemed, even
                    in the cradle.

Don't label my love with slogans;
My father can't be blamed
                    for my affection
Or lack of it;
ask him.
He won't understand you.

Don't sit on holy stones
                    as you,
Loving me
            and hating me, condemn.
There is no need for that.

I like to think that I, though
                    young it's true,
Know what
            I'm doing.

That I, once unhappy, am
Now
Quite sanely
        jubilant,
& that neither you
Nor I can
Deny
That no matter how
"Sick"
The basis
is
Of what we have,
What we *do* have
Is Good.

JOHANN

You look at me with children
In your eyes,
   Blond, blue-eyed
Teutons
Charmingly veiled
In bronze
   Got from me.

What would Hitler say?

I am brown-er
Than a jew
Being one step
Beyond that Colored scene.
You are the Golden Boy,
Shiny but bloody
And with that ancient martial tune
Only your heart is out of step—
You love.

But even knowing love
I shrink from you. Blond
And Black; it is too charged a combination.
Charged with past and present wars,
Charged with frenzy
and with blood

Dare I kiss your German mouth?
Touch the perfect muscles
Underneath the yellow shirt
Blending coolly
With your yellow
Hair?

I shudder at the whiteness
Of your hands.

Blue is too cold a color
For eyes.

But white, I think, is the color
Of honest flowers,

And blue is the color
Of the sky.

Come closer then and hold out to me
Your white and faintly bloodied hands.
I will kiss your German mouth
And will touch the helpless
White skin, gone red,
Beneath the yellow shirt.
I will rock the yellow head against
My breast, brown and yielding.

But I tell you, love,
There is still much to fear.
We have only seen the

First of wars
First of frenzies
First of blood.

Someday, perhaps, we will be
Made to learn
That blond and black
Cannot love.

But until that rushing day
I will not reject you.
I will kiss your fearful
German mouth.
And you—
Look at me boldly
With surging, brown-blond teutons
In your eyes.

THE SMELL

OF LEBANON

in balmy
  iconic
prague
I offered
my bosom
    to a wandering arab student
who spoke
much
of
Lebanon
    and
      his father's
        orchards

              it
          was near
          a castle
            near
          a river
            near
          the sun
            and
          warm

&
where he
bent
and kissed
 me
on the swelling
brown
smelled for
a short
    lingering
        time
of
  apples.

WARNING

To love a man wholly
love him
feet first
    head down
    eyes cold
    closed
in depression.

It is too easy to love
a surfer
white eyes
godliness &
         bronze
in the bright sun.

THE BLACK PRINCE

Very proud
he barely asked directions
to a nearby
hotel
      but no
      tired-eyed
      little village chief
      should spend his
      first night
      in chilly London
      alone.

MEDICINE

Grandma sleeps with
my sick
                grand-
pa so she
can get him
during the night
medicine
to stop
  the pain

      In
    the morning
      clumsily
        I
      wake
        them

Her eyes
look at me
from under-
                neath
his withered
arm

The
medicine
is all
in
her long
un-
braided
hair.

BALLAD OF

THE BROWN GIRL

i've got two
hundred
      dollars
the girl said
on her head
she wore a
school cap
—blue—
& brown she
looked no
more than
ten
but a freshman in
college?
well, hard
to tell—

i'll give you
'three hundred'
'fo' hunna'
'five wads of jack'

but "*mrs.* whatsyourname . . ."
the doctor says
with impatiently tolerant
eyes

you should *want*
it
you know . . .
talk it over with
your folks
you *may be*
        surprised. . . .

the next morning
her slender
neck broken
her note short
and of cryptic
collegiate
make—

      just

"Question—

did ever brown
daughter to black
father a white
baby
    take—?"

SUICIDE

First, suicide notes should be
(not long) but written
second,
all suicide notes
should be signed
in blood
by hand
and to the point—
that point being, perhaps,
that there is none.
Thirdly, if it is the thought
of rest that
fascinates
laziness should be admitted
in the clearest terms.
Then, all things done
ask those outraged
consider their happiest
summer
& tell if the days it
adds up to
is one.

EXCUSE

Tonight it is the wine (or not the wine)
or a letter from you (or not a letter from you)
I sit
listen to the complacency of the rain
write a poem, kill myself there

It brings less pain—

Tonight it rains, tomorrow will be bright
tomorrow I'll say "yesterday was the same
only the rain . . .

and my shoes too tight."

TO DIE

BEFORE ONE WAKES

MUST BE GLAD

to die before one
wakes
must be glad

(to the same extent
maybe
    that it is also
sad)

a slipping away
in glee
unobserved and
free
in the wide—

area felt spatially,
heart intact.

to die before one
wakes
must be joyous
full swing glorious
(rebellion)
(victory)
unremarked triumph

love letters untorn
foetal fears
unborn
monsters given
berth

(love unseen, guiltily,
as creation)
       (life "good")

to die before one
wakes
must be a dance

       (perhaps a jig)
       and visual-

skipping tunes of
color
across smirking
eyelids
happy bluely . . .
thought running gaily
out and out.

to die before one
wakes
must be
nice
(green little passions
red dying
into ice
spinningly
   (like a circus)

the blurred landscape
of the runner's
hurried
mile)
one's lips curving
sweetly
in one's most subtle smile.

EXERCISES ON

THEMES FROM LIFE

i

Speaking of death
and decay
It hardly matters
Which
Since both are on the
way, maybe—
to being daffodils.

ii

It is not about that
a poet I knew used
to say
speaking with haunted eyes
of liking and disliking—
Now I think
uncannily
of life.

iii

My nausea has nothing
to do
With the fact that
you love me

It is probably just
something I ate
at your mother's.

iv

To keep up a
passionate courtship
with a tree
one must be
completely mad
In the forest
in the dark one night
I lost my way.

v

If I were a patriot
I would kiss the flag
As it is,
Let us just go.

vi

My father liked very much
the hymns
in church
in the amen corner,
on rainy days
he would wake
himself up
to hear them.

vii

I like to see you try
to worm yourself
away from me
first you plead
your age
as if my young heart
felt any of the tiredness
in your bones . . .

viii

Making our bodies touch
across your breezy bed
how warm you are . . .
cannot we save our little
quarrel
until tomorrow?

ix

My fear of burial
is all tied up with
how used I am
to the spring . . . !

Books by Alice Walker
available in paperback editions
from Harcourt Brace Jovanovich, Publishers

Goodnight, Willie Lee, I'll See You in the Morning
In Love & Trouble
In Search of Our Mothers' Gardens
Once: Poems
Revolutionary Petunias and Other Poems
The Third Life of Grange Copeland
You Can't Keep a Good Woman Down